AGELESS INDIA - 5

art fact

AGELESS INDIA - 5

MONUMENTAL INDIA

Curated by
Abha Narain Lambah

Series Editor
MALVIKA SINGH

LIMITED
EDITIONS

AN IMPRINT OF
ACADEMIC FOUNDATION

INTRODUCTION TO THE SERIES

This series of Notebooks was conceived as a vibrant and energetic representation of India, manifesting images of her past and present, her remarkable and infinite civilisation with its endless layers of diversity merging and melding into one another, creating a fabric of seamless transitions laced with overlaps of buoyant contradictions that are often unpredictable and mysterious, allowing for flights of the imagination, and leaving 'room for wonder'.

Through the pages of *Ageless India*, this extraordinary and finely nuanced, ever-evolving and contemporary destination on earth, continues to draw into its complex unstitched folds, the many stories and experiences, the influences and ideas that emerge from a 'planet', continually revolving ecliptically on its firm axis, sharing experience and endorsing a sublime unity in exciting and invigorating diversity.

The voyeur in us can use these books to exchange notes, share ideas, articulate intangible reflections in words, and more, to leave them as 'memories' that can be savoured today, as well as in the years to come, by family and friends, to keep the connect of the past with the future alive.

Ageless India will showcase the personalised 'India' of men and women impassioned by her many 'plots' and 'sub-plots', using the skill of their hands and eyes to capture for posterity, her changing avatars, her multiple expressions. The series will be infinite...

Malvika Singh
New Delhi 2015

AGELESS INDIA - 5

MONUMENTAL INDIA

The material, man-made heritage of India rests in the extraordinary range of ancient and contemporary cities and historical forts; in the grand palaces and private *havelis*, the mansions and homes; in the temples, shrines and places of worship dedicated to all faiths and religions; in the gardens and tombs; even great institutions of learning. The architectural expertise spanning millenia, embellished with fine surface decoration representing time, age and purpose, makes this legacy of India unsurpassed, precious and fragile. This collection of photographs by conservation architect Abha Narain Lambah establishes the urgent need for conservation and preservation. India must take ownership of her varied and layered past to conquer the future. This compendium is merely the tip of a formidable *khazana*.

Series Editor
MALVIKA SINGH

Ajanta Panoramic, Aurangabad

Panoramic view of the Ajanta Caves, a spectacular ensemble of ancient rock cut caves of Buddhist *chaityas* and *viharas* and a UNESCO World Heritage Site. The View Point was probably the location from where an officer of the Madras Army accidentally stumbled upon and rediscovered the lost caves in 1819.

lai Darwaza and Qutb Minar,
)elhi

'he architectural legacy of the
slamic Sultanate in Delhi is a
nulti-coloured mosaic that owes
:s patronage to 35 sultans,
ontributing to the creation of a
istinctive style of Indo-Islamic
rchitecture that progressed
rom an earlier architecture
f demolition and recycling to
ater monumental constructions
ncompassing the religious,
ecular and sepulchral. Among
he icons of the architecture
f the Sultanates is the
pectacular composition of the
utb Minar built by Qutbu'd-
in Aibak and his successor
ltutmish and the Alai Darwaza
uilt by Sultan Ala-ud-din Khilji.
he Alai Darwaza is a gateway,
ot a sepulchral monument
nd yet it remains a key link
n the development of tomb
ypology, successfully combin-
ng engineering prowess with
sophisticated architectural
esthetic.

lbert Hall, Jaipur

'he Albert Hall in Jaipur is mong the most iconic buildings f the Indo Saracenic genre hat attempted to superimpose n a symmetrical Western plan, ll the trappings of Oriental rnamentation, often blending Iughal, Rajput or Islamic ele- nents to create a 'pan Indian tyle'. Sir Swinton Jacob's *Jey- ore Portfolio of Architectural)etails*, became a veritable atalogue of *jaalis*, *chhatris*, omes, lintels, plinths and opings. Jacob's most ambitious roject, the Albert Hall was ompleted for the Maharaja of aipur in 1887. Indo Saracenic rchitecture held its sway over he early 20th century, with the ange of public buildings, royal alaces of the local Maharajas, nuseums, post offices, educa- ional institutions and even a hurch being built in this style.

Anand Bhavan and Swaraj Bhavan, Allahabad

An icon of the freedom movement, Anand Bhavan was built by Motilal Nehru and served as the home to three future Prime Ministers of India. The house served as the venue for many meetings of the Indian National Congress and hosted some of the greatest names in the nationalist movement. Until the construction of Anand Bhawan, the Nehru residence was the building now known as Swaraj Bhawan. However, Swaraj Bhavan was originally named Anand Bhavan in 1900, untill it got its new name when Motilal Nehru gifted it to the Congress in 1930. The names Anand Bhavan and Swaraj Bhavan are thus interchangeable until 1930 when the Nehrus moved to the new building that was then renamed Anand Bhavan.

Bombay Gothic—The Victorian Architecture of Mumbai

Among the most iconic buildings of the 19th century, the Municipal Head Offices and the Victoria Terminus Station were both designed by the famous architect Frederick William Stevens. Completed in 1893, the Municipal Corporation Building is among the finest example of a localised Victorian Gothic, style artfully blending pointed arches and cinquefoils with bulbous domes to produce a monumental hybrid of the Indo Gothic architectural genre. The structure has some grand interior spaces, the Corporation Hall with its stained glass windows and wooden panelling being among the most impressive. It is currently undergoing an ambitious restoration. (Image Credit: Krishna Iyer for Abha Narain Lambah Associates.)

Brihadisvara Temple, Thanjavur

The Great Living Chola Temple of Brihadisvara Temple at Thanjavur, was declared by UNESCO as a World Heritage Site in 1987. One of the three great Chola temples of South India, this 1,000 year old temple complex represents the zenith of architectural development of the Dravida temple form.

Previous page: Tomb of Sufi Saint Salim Chishti, Fatehpur Sikri

In the imperial city of Fatehpur Sikri, the exquisite white marble edifice of the Sufi Saint Salim Chishti (1478–1572) is set like a precious pearl in the urban composition of red sandstone buildings within the *sahn* of the Jama Masjid. Its intricately carved marble *jaalis* are fine as lace, and the serpentine brackets exhibit the sophistication of Mughal craftsmanship.

Charminar, Hyderabad

Charminar's pioneering design with its four symmetrical minarets even preceded the use of four minarets by the Mughals. Charminar, with its strong symmetry of four minars, constructed in 1591 falls between the construction of Humayun's tomb (1562-1571) wihout minars, to the distinct inclusion of four minars in the design of Akbar's sepulchral gateway at Sikandra (1613). This Indian prototype of a monumental structure framed by four minars is thus first established at Charminar and is subsequently followed by the four corner minars in Jehangir's Tomb at Lahore with its final culmination in the Taj Mahal framed by four minars.

Convocation Hall, Mumbai

Designed by the famous British architect Sir George Gilbert Scott, the Convocation Hall and University Library buildings are the only structures in India designed by the leading Victorian architect. Since Gilbert Scott never found the time to visit India, all the details about Indian climatic conditions and requirements of the University had to be settled by correspondence. Construction of the 104 feet long, 44 feet wide and 63 feet high Victorian Neo Gothic structure was completed in 1874 through a generous grant by Sir Cowasjee Jehangir, whose statue is placed in the foreground. The Convocation Hall was carefully restored in 2006 and won an UNESCO Asia Pacific Award of Distinction in 2007.

Previous page: Taj Detail

A detail of the exquisite pietra dura and marble bas relief panel at the entrance of the Taj Mahal with floral and foliate motifs is a spectacula illustration of Mughal craftsmanship.

Previous page:
Ellora, Aurangabad

The Kailasnath Temple at Ellora is one of the most breathtaking sites in the world. Carved out of igneous rockface, the temple is a monumental vision in stone, a monolithic piece of sculpture carved top down, to craft a Shaivite temple complex. Inscribed by UNESCO as a World Heritage Site, the caves at Ellora can be divided into three groups viz., Buddhist, Brahmanical and Jain. Chronologically they are spread over the period of six centuries from 6th to 12th century AD.

Previous page: Falaknuma, Hyderabad

A jewel among all the palatial residences of Hyderabad, the Falaknuma Palace was an attempt at creating a fantastic architectural vision true to its name—"*Falaknuma*" or "Like Paradise". The palace was constructed over a period of seven years and it covers a total area of 9,39,712 square metres. The telephone and electrical system was introduced in 1883 by Osler and the palace had one of the largest electrical switchboards in India. Built by Vikar-ul-Umra, the fifth Amir of the Paigah dynasty in the late 19th century, the grand complex was initially meant for his own use, but was later acquired by the Nizam of Hyderabad Mahboob Ali Khan in 1897. Falaknuma palace is today amongst the most luxurious heritage hotels of India.

Diwan-e-Khas, Fatehpur Sikri

Perhaps the most iconic interior spaces of Mughal India is the Diwan-e-Khas at Fatehpur Sikri, the Hall of Private Audience of Emperor Akbar. The monolithic red sandstone column supporting a bouquet of carved brackets holds up the central throne and four centred passages that were famed for once having supported Great Mughal and his courtiers—witness to inter-religious discussions and the foundation of Din-e-Ilahi, Akbar's own view of a state religion. The imperial city of Fatehpur Sikri was founded in 1569, and served as the capital of the Mughal Empire for a brief period of 14 years. Akbar's imperial city of Fatehpur Sikri is the crystalisation of the greatest Mughal emperor's architectural vision in stone.

hurches of Goa

nce known as the Rome of the
rient, Goa has some of the
nest Portuguese churches and
asilicas dating as far back as
510. Among these stunning
hurches are the Sé Catedral
e Santa Catarina, the Saint
atherine's Chapel, the Church
f Saint Francis of Assisi, the
asílica do Bom Jesus, the
hurch of Our Lady of the Ro-
ary. These churches with lofty
terior spaces established the
enchmark for the Manueline,
annerist and Baroque forms
Asia.

·olconde, Puducherry

he archetype of modernism in ndia, Golconde in Puduch-rry is an icon of modernism. esigned by architects Antonin aymond and George Nakashi-na, this building constructed n 1942 is the pioneering xample of modern architec-ure in India and pre dates orbusier's constructions in handigarh and Ahmedabad by wo decades. Golconde was the rst reinforced, cast-in-place oncrete building in India and s bold form, exposed concrete, un breakers and introverted ndscape became the prototype or a generation of modern uildings in India. Golconde emains timeless in its stark mplicity as an uncompromis-ng architectural icon.

Gwalior Fort

Gwalior has had a succession of rulers including the Rajputs, Mughals and Marathas. It rose to great prominence during the period of Tomar Rajputs between 1398 and 1518, particularly during the reign of Raja Man Singh (r.1486-1517). The formidable fortification of Gwalior built by the Tomar Rajputs has been witness to fierce battles, *jauhars*, courage and treachery, as well as the incarceration of a Sikh Guru. The lofty sandstone ramparts embellished with azure tiles, cover a length of two miles and have earned the reputation of having been among the invincible forts of India. The architecture of the fort earned it the title, "pearl among the fortresses of Hind" by Mughal emperor Babur and the famous 15th century palace of Raja Mansingh built for his Gujar Queen Mrignayani inspired Akbar's architecture.

Halvad Palace, Gujarat

Tucked away in the Surendranagar district of Gujarat, Halvad is an architectural gem. The Halvad palace stands on the edge of a lake and ensconces an introverted courtyard with a formal garden at the centre of which stands a multi-tiered octagonal tower with viewing *jharokhas*. Framing the courtyard are exquisitely carved wooden colonnades supporting wooden brackets that are an ode to the superior craftsmanship of Gujarati artisans. Though owned by the erstwhile royal family of Dhrangadhara, this palace is among the rare cases of privately owned monuments under National Protection.

Hampi Tank, Karnataka

Integral to the planning of monumental temple complexes in Vijayanagara, were water tanks that formed a part of the ritualistic practices. The water tanks connected to Krishna Temple and Vithhala are some of the most beautiful water structures in Southern India.

Previous page:
Viceregal Lodge, Shimla

Completed in 1888, the Viceregal Lodge was designed by Henry Irwin in the Elizabethan Gothic with its expansive estate, richly panelled Burma teak wood interiors and Maple furniture imported from England spelling the height of the Raj in India.

Igu—Buddhist Temples of Ladakh

Perched precariously on steep mountains, these indefatigable earth constructions covered in white *markhala* clay, the Ladakhi Buddhist temples and monasteries of Igu, Hemis, Basgo, Spituk, Shey are among the most spectacular icons of religious architecture in India.

Iltutmish's Tomb, Delhi

The creation of Islamic architectural forms for the Delhi Sultanate was propelled by as much political as architectural motive. Announcing a clean break from the deeply rooted Hindu and Jaina trabeate traditions of building was a means of reinforcing the identity of the Sultanate. The tomb of Sultan Iltutmish is key to the understanding of this architectural development. While attempting Islamic forms of squinches and domes, its builders struggled with establishing a truly arcuate construction model. The challenge was to translate arcuate forms into the traditional trabeate construction system of the Hindu artisans, a struggle amply demonstrated in the initial experiments with false arches in the screens of the Quwwat al Islam, as well as the failed dome of Iltumish's tomb. It took the Delhi Sultanate nearly a century to create the true arch to give structural validity to Islamic form. Even the failed dome of Iltutmish's tomb is thus an icon of the evolutionary process of architecture of the Indian Sultanates.

Previous page: Jaisalmer Fort, Rajasthan

The medieval desert outpost of Jaisalmer fort stands on the edge of the Thar desert of Rajasthan. Protected within its massive fortifications of golden sandstone is a medieval city of richly ornamented *havelis*, Rajput palaces, ancient temples and a thousand year old settlement. The historic fort of Jaisalmer was founded by Rao Jaisal in 1156 as a political move from his more vulnerable capital at Ludherva, making it the oldest living fortified city in Rajasthan. Sonar Kila (Golden Fort as its name made famous by Satyajit Ray), its gleaming golden sandstone fortifications were strategically positioned on one of the central Asian trade routes, and made fortunes for Rajputs and Jain merchants on caravans laden with silk, opium and spices in the medieval times.

'aisalmer, Rajasthan

he Rajasthani craftsmen of 'aisalmer crafted the finest ierced stone screens for he palaces and havelis of 'aisalmer. View of the carved tone *jharokhas* of the palace uildings overlooking Dusshera howk within the fortified own.

Previous page:
Blue City, Jodhpur

The city of Jodhpur in Rajasthan with its dense urban fabric of winding streets lined with *bazaars* and *havelis* is often called the 'blue city' for its houses of Brahmins washed with *neel*, indigo infused in the lime wash. The Mehrangarh fort offers a bird's-eye view of the city.

Shah-e-Hamdan, Srinagar

The Shah-e-Hamdan mosque, also known as the Khanqah mosque, is located in the heart of the old city of Srinagar, on the banks of river Jhelum between the Fatehkadal and Zainakadal bridges. Built by Shah Sikandar to commemorate the visit of Hazrat Mir Syed Ali Hamdani, better known as Shah Hamdan in 1372 and 1383, the single storeyed mosque was originally built in 1394 AD near the Hujra Khas. The shrine was damaged by fire and rebuilt twice, in 1479 and later in 1734. The mosque is an icon of Islamic architecture in the valley, with decorative *khatam-bandi* panels and intricate woodwork.

Khajuraho

The temples of Khajuraho with their towering *shikharas* with tiered *urusringras* are the archetypes of the North Indian Hindu temple form. Built by the Chandela Rajputs, these stone temples symbolise the apogee of temple form and sculptural exuberence. The Khandarya Mahadeo Temple and the Lakshmana Temple are perhaps the best examples of this style and masterpieces of Indian art and architecture.

SUMRTSEK TEMPLE
SUMTSEK TEMPLE

lchi, Ladakh

he *chos-khor* or shrines
f Alchi Gompa in Ladakh
ate to the 10th-11th Century
nd are ascribed to Rinchen
angpo. The shrines of Alchi
re amongst the most iconic of
adakhi sites, blending early
ashmiri building influences.
ney hold within them, a wealth
f spectacular wall paintings,
mong the oldest surviving in
ne region in predominant blue,
hites and red ochre colours.

:anheri, Mumbai

ocated within the Sanjay andhi National Park in :umbai, Kānheri is one of the ıajor rock-cut complexes in the 'estern Ghāts and comprises ıore than a hundred caves. his cave complex is referred to s 'Krishnagiri' or 'Kanhagiri' ı ancient inscriptions. The site as under active habitation for ıore than a thousand years. umerous chaityas and viharas ın be seen here excavated in ıe steep scarps of the hills hich form a key link in the ıain of development of rock ıt architecture in the world.

Lal Bagh Palace, Indore

The Lal Bagh Palace has among the most significant historic interiors among the palaces of the erstwhile rulers of princely states. The flamboyant interiors of the Holkar palace of Lal Bagh in Indore is a celebration of the Baroque, a style adopted for their new palaces by both the Scindias and Holkars, Maratha rulers. Planning for the site was commenced in the reign of King Tukoji Rao II (1844-1886). His successor Shivaji Rao Holkar (1886-1902) constructed the main Lalbag palace as a small garden house in 1890s but it was however, Tukoji Rao III (1902-1925) who contributed the most to the opulent interiors.

WAY TO
& BALCONY
& BALCONY

Liberty Cinema, Mumbai

The 1930s in Bombay were the heady days of a new global aesthetic, including influences in jazz, cinema, architecture and design. Art Deco percolated through Europe as travel by steam liners opened the floodgates to international travel. Mumbai's Art Deco development was manifested through its iconic cinema halls and apartment buildings. The interiors of Liberty Cinema carefully preserved under the watchful eye of its owner Nazir Hoosein are amongst the finest surviving Art Deco interiors.

Lothal, Gujarat

One of the world's first urban civilisations, the Indus Valley Civilisation was emblematic of an extensive urban culture 4,600 years ago. The Indus Valley Civilisation, covering an area of more than a million and a half square kilometres consists of a vast range of urban settlements unified by the common thread of trade and commerce, which led to uniformity of town planning and material products. Lothal comprises a critical component of the Indus Valley culture. The presence of the unique and massive scientifically designed brick lined dockyard at Lothal reveals the crucial role played by this Harappan port-city in the Indo-Sumerian trade. It comprised of one of the most sophisticated urban layouts, with outstanding construction methodology of the dock along with rigorous planning norms for sewage and drainage systems, envisaged over 4,000 years ago. Lothal along with Dholavira, is an outstanding example of the quality of life, urban town plan and social structure of the lost Harappan culture.

Maluti Temples, Jharkhand

Nestled in a remote village in Jharkhand, the teracotta temples of Maluti are an ensemble of 60 temples which belong to the period between 17th and 19th centuries. Located in clusters, these temples built in the indigenous Bengali style of architecture, with exquisite terracotta work, display mastery of the local craftsmen, who created these beautiful houses of worship.

Previous page:
Mehrangarh Fort, Jodhpur

The iconic image of the Mehrangarh Fort atop a rocky hill dominating the skyline of Jodhpur defines the quintessential image of a Rajput fortress. One of the largest forts in Rajasthan, Mehrangarh is the home of the Rathore Rajputs and nestles within its formidable walls, some of the finest examples of Rajput architecture, spanning over 500 years of architectural development over generations of rulers.

Previous page:
Moorish Mosque, Kapurthala

The Francophile Maharaja of Kapurthala Jagatjit Singh's patronage resulted in the construction of a unique mosque in the heart of the princely state of Punjab. The Moorish Mosque also known as Jama Masjid locally is a grand mosque, suitable perhaps more in the Moroccan desert than the plains of Punjab. Built in 1930 by a French Architect Manteaux, it draws its design inspiration from the great Kutubbiya mosque, at Marakesh in Morocco. The original design included the mosque proper, a garden and orchards of citrus fruits and peaches that contributed some revenue for its upkeep.

Qutb Shahi Tombs, Hyderabad

'he Qutb Shahi dynasty
1518-1687) was one of the five
rominent Islamic sultan-
.tes that emerged in Deccan
ndia following the downfall
f the Bahmanis in the 16th
entury. Seven Qutb Shahi
ulers reigned for nearly 170
ears and successfully resisted
Mughal attacks till 1687 A.D.
.s the royal tomb complex of
he last Deccani sultanate to
e absorbed in the expanding
Mughal Empire, the tombs
resent an exceptional example
f an Indo-Islamic dynastic
ecropolis, bearing Persian and
ocal Deccani influences.

Vithhala Temple, Hampi

Amongst the most iconic temples in India, the Vithala Temple in Hampi with its massive *mahadwaras* of stone, brick and stucco, the stone *ratha* chariot and stone columns that sound like musical instruments when struck, is the epitome of temple architecture. Its proportions, planning and the recently excavated *bazaar* that frames the urban axis leading to the temple make it truly worthy of its UNESCO World Heritage status.

Santiniketan, West Bengal

Founded by Rabindranath Tagore in 1901 and located in Bengal's rural hinterland, Santiniketan represents the distillation of Rabindranath Tagore's life, philosophy and greatest works through his lifetime and the continuing legacy of his unique model of education through a living institution and architectural ensemble. And while many of Tagore's greatest art and literary works bear a unique association with Santiniketan, it can be argued that his model of an Indian education through the revival of the *tapoban* tradition and humanist ideology finds its greatest reflection in Santiniketan, thus making it Tagore's greatest work. In his last letter to Mahatma Gandhi, Tagore wrote *"Visva Bharati is like a vessel carrying the cargo of my life's best treasure and I hope it may claim special care from my countrymen for its preservation"*.

Previous page: Sasaram, Bihar

Had Sher Shah Suri's rule as emperor of Hindustan not abruptly come to an end due to a freak accident, perhaps the Mughal dynasty could not have found an entry back into India after the rout of Humayun's army and his seeking asylum in Persia. Sher Shah Suri was a courageous general and a visionary. His ideas of connecting India through better highways and administrative reforms were later copied by Akbar. Not hailing royal stock, he chose to build monumental mausoleums for his father, grandfather and himself in Narnaul and Sasaram. His own tomb at Sasaram set in the middle of a water body is the epitome of Pathan architecture.

supalgarh, Odisha

ating to 3rd Century BCE, the
ıcient city of Sisupalgarh
defined by a rampart and
oat that encloses the area
130 ha. The rampart is well
eserved under a mound and
ands enclosing a
rmal square shape with
ght gates regularly spaced
ong four sides. Excavated for
e first time in 1948 by the
chaeological Survey of India
determine its history and
aracter, the second series of
cavations were only
rried out recently in 2008-09.
e site was subsequently
cavated in 1950 (by Dr B.K.
apar) and then from 2005
2009 by Dr Rabi Mohanty
d Dr Monika Smith. The lofty
one pillars stand testimony to
e monumental ancient citadel
Sisupalgarh, a site severely
der threat from unplanned
velopment.

ok, Leh

mong the most iconic and nique royal residences of ndia is the living palace of ok, home to the members of e erstwhile Namgyal rulers f Ladakh. After the sacking f Leh by the Dogra army, the uling family moved to Stok nd built a new palace in the aditional Tibeto-Ladakhi style f multi-tiered mud walls and ooden balconies. Stok is iconic ot only for its architectural niqueness, reminiscent of otala Palace in Tibet, but also s a royal palace lived in by the ounger royals of the Namgyal amily—Raja Jigmed and Rani alzas Namgyal and their hildren.

Taj Mahal Palace Hotel, Mumbai

Built in 1903 by Jamshedji Tata to give India its greatest luxury hotel, urban myths associated with the Taj Mahal Palace Hotel range from this being built by Tata after he was disallowed entry to the Whites only Watson's Hotel—and of the architect committing suicide after the building was built in reverse of its riginal plan. Both these myths remain strongly contested, but it is undoubtedly among the nest Indo Saracenic buildings f the early 20th century. The building once again became a part of Mumbai's legends due to the fateful terrorist attack of 26/11 that led to many deaths nd massive destruction. This hotograph was taken the ay after the Terrorist attack ended, with police women ordoning off the area and moke having blackened the stone towers.

Taj Mahal, Agra

The Taj Mahal seen from the Bagh e Mehtab on the opposite bank of the Yamuna.

Previous page: Taj Panoramic

View of the Taj Mahal, the world's most famous mausoleum and a UNESCO World Heritage Site seen from across the Yamuna. The perfect proportions and juxtaposition of white marble and red sandstone makes for an incomparable architectural composition.

Temples of Kancheepuram, Tamil Nadu

Kancheepuram in Tamil Nadu has been a major site of pilgrimage for Shaivaites, Vaishnavites, Jains and Buddhists over the centuries. Hailed as the 'City of a Thousand Temples', it is home to the Kanchi Math, founded by Adi Shankaracharya and is known as *Dakshin Kashi*. Considered as one of the foremost '*Shakti Peethas*', it is among the four *dhams* of Hinduism and is also a renowned cultural repository of South India, in addition to being one of the greatest centres of textile weaving—home to the famous Kanjeevaram saree we aving tradition.

Victoria Memorial, Kolkata

The swansong of English architect Sir William Emerson and the crystalisation of Lord Curzon's vision in white marble, Victoria Memorial is among the most iconic of British colonial buildings in India. In keeping with Calcutta's neoclassicism, this monumental memorial to the longest reigning empress of India—Queen Victoria remains a landmark of Kolkata and amongst the finest colonial edifices.

'ictoria Terminus, Mumbai

Vith its grand verticality, uttresses, spires, towers, argoyles, turrets, Venetian alconies, the use of angular, ointed forms and large, high eiling interior spaces, the 'ictoria Terminus station now enamed Chhatrapati Shivaji 'erminus, is the most spectacu-ar railway station in the world. esigned by Frederick William tevens in the Neo-Gothic tyle, the Terminus building s among the masterpieces of 'ictorian engineering. It is lso stylistically influenced by he architecture of the Indian ub-continent, evident in the etailing of its domed cupolas nd corner spires. The station nd offices were built by the reat Indian Peninsula Railway nd completed in May 1888, t a cost of Rupees 2.6 million. he station was opened earlier or trains on 1st January 1882 nd is among the oldest func-ioning railway stations in the orld. (Image Credit: Krishna yer for Abha Narain Lambah ssociates).

Previous page:
Karauli Fort, Rajasthan

Karauli in Rajasthan was once the part of Matsya kingdom that was ruled by the Meenas and later the Rajputs. The town dates from 1348 CE, and is situated in a position naturally defended by ravines on the north and east, while it is further protected by a great wall. Karauli fort was founded by Maharaja Arjun Dev Yadav in 1348 and is built of the local reddish sandstone. The Maharaja's palace has some stunning painted chambers.

Previous page:
Doraha Panoramic, Punjab

The Mughal Sarai at Doraha in Punjab forms an integral part of the chain of *carvansarais* built along the old Mughal highway between Agra and Lahore. The *caravansarais* represent a unique secular building type within the vocabulary of Indian Islamic architecture. Altogether more than twenty Mughal Sarais stand along the old Mughal highway between Agra and Lahore, a distance of more than four hundred miles. Sarai Doraha is one of the most spectacular of the Mughal *Sarais*, built in *Lakhori* brick with ornamentation in incised plaster, glazed tiles and wall paintings. As its name implies (doraha means “two roads”), the Sarai is situated at the intersection of two main routes along the Mughal highway. It is held by most scholars that the Doraha Sarai dates to the early years of Jahangir’s reign, a full decade before Sarai Nur Mahal. (Image Credit: Krishna Iyer for Abha Narain Lambah Associates).

Previous page:
Virupaksha Panoramic

The only living temple to survive the mass destruction of Vijaynagara by the combined forces of the Deccan Sultanate confederacy in the 16th century, Virupaksha Temple is the temple of Lord Virupaksha—the Shaivite deity of Hampi. Hampi, the site of the richest city of the South during the rule of the Vijayanagara empire under Krishnadevaraya, is rooted in the sacred mythology of Pampa, the Tungabhadra river. Each year, the Ratha festival celebrates the wedding of Pampa to Virupaksha—a celestial marriage between Lord Shiva and the sacred river. Also known as Virupakshapura and Vijayanagar, Hampi is inscribed as a UNESCO World Heritage Site.

Previous page: Sri Ranganath Temple, Pushkar

It is rather surprising to encounter a South Indian temple in the middle of Pushkar in Rajasthan, but the Sri Ranganath Temple is a unique example of the fusion of Rajasthani and South Indian temple forms with the patronage of Marwari traders who settled in Hyderabad and Deccan and continued their link with their ancestral lands. (Image Credit: Krishna Iyer for Abha Narain Lambah Associates).

Previous page: Ajanta Caves, Aurangabad

View of the rock cut caves of Ajanta nestled in the spectacular sweep of the horse shoe geological formation of the Sahyadri mountains. Ancient Buddhist monks would have carefully selected this site for its oneness with nature.

Previous page: Red Fort, Delhi

It is an act of political symbolism and through careful design that the Prime Minister of India delivers his Independence Day speech from the ramparts of the Red Fort. This Mughal fort built as the political centre of Shahjehan's imperial city has stood as the symbol of power for over 350 years—first as the Mughal capital city, then the scene of the 1857 War of Independence and finally as the symbol of free India. UNESCO declared the Red Fort as a UNESCO World Heritage Site in acknowledgement of its unique historical and architectural significance.

Previous page:
Amer Fort, Jaipur

Embodying the zenith of Rajput architecture and marking the synthesis of Rajput and Mughal planning principles, the Amer Fort forms a formidable defensive fortification system over the Aravalli hills and valleys to create an undefeatable citadel. Built by the Kachchwaha Rajput rulers, it exemplifies the maturation of the Rajput Mughal architectural style from the 17th century. Amer is inscribed as a UNESCO World Heritage Site as part of the Serial Nomination of the Hill Forts of Rajasthan.

Victoria Memorial, Kolkata

The interiors of the Victoria Memorial are designed to awe and inspire. The central rotunda is capped by a lofty dome that rises above the central statue of Queen Victoria, bathing it with natural day light streaming through the clerestory windows.

Previous page:
The Basgo Citadel, Ladakh

The historic citadel of Basgo, once the seat of the Namgyal rulers of Ladakh is a spectacular vision of earth constructions perched on top of the hill. The citadel's battered earth walls nestle Buddhist temples from the 15th and 16th century. The complex underwent a 3 year restoration project partnered by the World Monuments Fund, Basgo Village Welfare Committee and the Namgyal Institute of Research on Ladakhi Art & Culture and won the UNESCO Asia Pacific Heritage Award of Excellence in 2007.

Bodh Gaya

Bodh Gaya is revered by Buddhists as one of the holiest places on earth. The 5th Century temple stands at the spot of the Enlightenment of Lord Buddha. The Mahabodhi Temple was first built by Emperor Asoka in the 3rd century B.C., and the present temple dates from the 5th–6th centuries. It is one of the earliest Buddhist temples built entirely in brick, from the late Gupta period and it is considered to have had significant influence in the development of brick architecture over the centuries. The Mahabodhi Temple Complex was inscribed by UNESCO as a World Heritage Site in 2002.

Mahabodhi Temple, Bodh Gaya

Young Monks performing the sacred *pradakshina* around the Mahabodhi temple and tracing Buddha's steps along the Ratna Cancama.

Champaner, Gujarat

The medieval monuments of Champaner represent the syncretism of Islamic and Hindu forms that reached a crescendo of architectural evolution in the Islamic Sultanate of Gujarat. The 16th century monuments include lofty mosques, minarets and gateways ornamented with exquisitely carved stone *jaalis* in a celebration of local craftsmanship. On the 7th July 2004, Champaner-Pavagadh Archaeological Park was inscribed by UNESCO in the list of World Heritage Sites.

Interiors of the Convocation Hall, Mumbai

The Interiors of the Convocation Hall in Mumbai are the epitome of Victorian Gothic, complete with stained glass windows, gas lights, Minton encaustic tiles and gilded wrought iron railings.
(Image Credit: Rajesh Vora for Abha Narain Lambah Associates).

Previous page: Golden Temple, Amritsar

The spiritual centre of Sikhism, Sri Darbar Sahib in Amritsar stands as an icon of Sikhism and is an architectural masterpiece. Standing in the centre of the holy tank Amrit Sarovar, the foundation stone for the building was laid by Hazrat Mian Mir ji, embodying the egalitarian spirit of Sikhism. Gleaming in the reflective pool, the Golden Temple is a synthesis of Hindu and Islamic architectural elements to create a unique Sikh architectural vocabulary.

Iemis, Leh

'layed out to great dramatic
ffect, the masked dances of the
Iemis Festival make this mon-
stery courtyard come to life.
'he Hemis festival is dedicated
o Lord Padmasambhava (Guru
impoche) and is celebrated
hrough the dances at Hemis
Ionastery. A living monument,
Iemis remains one of the most
conic of the Buddhist monas-
eries of Upper Indus.

Hemis, Leh

Among the most iconic monasteries of Ladakh is the Hemis monastery, with its association with the Drukpa lineage and royal patronage from the Namgyal ruling family for centuries. Within the complex, the most iconic statue is that of Guru Rimpoche, Lord Padmasambhava who introduced Tantrik Buddhism to the region. The vibrant colours of mineral and natural colours bring the interior come to life.

Previous page:
Itmad ud Daula, Agra

The Taj Mahal could not have been the architectural marvel it is celebrated as, had it not been for the experimentation with decorative stonework and pietra dura that was perfected in the tomb of Itmad ud Daula. Lovingly built for her father Mirza Ghiyath Beg, the Prime Minister to Emperor Jehangir by the indefatigable queen Noor Jehan, this mausoleum bears the stamp of royal patronage and became the text book for later builders of the Taj. This tomb built between 1622 and 1628 heralds the transition in imperial Mughal buildings from the preference towards red sandstone, to the pure white Makrana marble.

Jaunpur

Beginning as an off shoot of the imperial Tughlaq style, the architecture of the Sharqis matured into a stylised sophistication, creating a distinct identity within the vocabulary of Islamic architecture. Sloping batten walls, ogee arches with rose bud ornamentation, recessed pylons and the illogical principle of lintels supporting arched openings are visible signs of a Tughlaq origin. In turn, the Sharqi buildings demonstrated a sound understanding of structural engineering, building lofty vaults and monumental gateways that gave a distinct character to the *Sharqi* style. The Jami Masjid is among the five royal Sharqi mosques of Jaunpur that capture the architectural expression of Jaunpur's rich medieval past.

JB

Previous page:
Lomas Rishi, Gaya

The earliest example of rock cut architecture in India, the Lomas Rishi cave in Gaya District of Bihar dates from the Mauryan period and forms the archetype for the chaitya halls of later more ambitious projects. Its arched shaped facade imitates contemporary timber buildings of ancient India and is testimony to the forms of ancient Indian architecture. The Lomas Rishi cave along with the Karan Chaupar, Sudama and Visva Zopri caves forms the group of Barabar caves.

विश्रामघाट
VISHRAM GHAT

Previous page: Pushkar

Pushkar...the city of Lord Brahma with its temples dotted along the lakeside ghats is a spiritual centre and an architectural gem.

Previous page: Quila Mubarak, Patiala

The Quila was built by the founder of the Sikh dynasty of Patiala, Raja Ala Singh who established his political capital at Patiala in 1763. The Quila continued to be added to and embellished by the successors of Raja Ala Singh for over a century. From the 1840s, Patiala rulers began constructing palaces outside the confines of the fortified city but the sacred *jyot* of Baba Ala Singh, brought from *Jwalamukhi* has remained lit in the core of the Quila Androon long after the successive rulers moved their residence out of the Quila. (Image Credit: Krishna Iyer for Abha Narain Lambah Associates).

Agra Red Fort

View of the ramparts and Musamman Burj, the great Mughal citadel of Agra Fort. The deposed Mughal emperor Shah Jehan was held captive here for the last days of his life by his son Aurangzeb. Agra Fort is inscribed as a UNESCO World Heritage Site as among the most spectacular forts of the world.

Rashtrapati Bhavan, New Delhi

Designed by Edwin Lutyens as the official residence of the Viceroy in India, the monumentality of Rashtrapati Bhavan is as much owed to its carefully calibrated setting on the top of Raisina Hill, flanked by the North and South Block of Herbert Baker's Secretariat buildings, as its selection of red and buff sandstone—reminiscent of imperial Mughal edifices and its lofty architectural proportions. The use of Indian motifs such as elephants, temple bells, the Sanchi stupa creates an interplay of the West and East that make this building truly iconic.

Previous page:
Municipal Head Office, Mumbai

Designed by the famous architect Frederick William Stevens, the Municipal Head Office building is surmounted with a lofty dome. Below this, is another dome, spectacular in its composition, crowning the central staircase. It is gilded in gold leaf, with a central inverted floret blending Indian and Neo Gothic architectural motifs.

Chowmahalla Palace, Hyderabad

The palace of the Nizam of Hyderabad, Chowmahalla Palace is spread over a vast estate in the heart of Hyderabad city—close to Charminar and Mecca Masjid. The palaces were built in two disctinct phases, the older section of Neo Classical European buildings around a central formal garden and a later section in the Indo Islamic style. The Afzal Mahal Palace with stunning European interiors is among the many palaces painstakingly restored under the watchful eye of Princess Esra and thrown open to the public. The conservation work won a UNESCO Asia Pacific Heritage Conservation Award of Merit in 2010.

Mani Bhavan, Mumbai

Built in the first decade of the 20th century, Mani Bhavan was home to Mahatma Gandhi during his stay in Bombay from 1917 to 1934 and played a pivotal role in the freedom struggle. This icon of the non voilent struggle for *Swaraj* was witness to many politically significant events such as the aunching of the Satyagraha Movement in March 1919, andhi's historic fast from 9th to 22nd November 1922 nd the decision to launch the ivil Disobedience for *Swaraj*. Mahatma Gandhi was arrested n his tent on the terrace of Mani Bhavan in the early hours f the morning of 4th January, 932. The building is presently n the care of the Mani Bhavan andhi Sangrahalaya.

Index

ABHA NARAIN LAMBAH is a practicing conservation architect with eight UNESCO Asia Pacific Heritage Conservation Award citations to her credit. She is the recipient of the Sanskriti Award, Eisenhower Fellowship and Charles Wallace Fellowship, and has been consultant to World Monuments Fund, Global Heritage Fund, Deccan Foundation and ICCROM.

Abha's work ranges from World Heritage Sites of Ajanta Caves and Bodh Gaya to award winning conservation of 15th Century temples in Hampi and Ladakh. Her architectural practice includes historic palaces and museums across India, to temples, forts, caravan serais and ancient monuments in Andhra Pradesh, Jharkhand, Madhya Pradesh, Odisha, Rajasthan, Tamil Nadu, Uttar Pradesh and West Bengal. She has advised on conservation of colonial buildings such as the Raj Bhavan and Indian Museum Kolkata, Teen Murti House and Bikaner House in New Delhi. She has been involved with the conservation of many of Mumbai's 19th century colonial structures and has authored conservation master plans for Viceregal Lodge Shimla and Government House Kolkata and Nainital.

MALVIKA SINGH, publisher of the monthly journal Seminar, is a well known columnist.

Malvika initiated and edited the India magazine, the first of it genre, that explored the many facets of India, her people and cultures. She has authored several books: *Perpetua City*; *Bhutan Through the Lens of the King*; *New Delhi: Making of a Capital*; *Delhi: India in One City*; and *Snowdon's India*. She has edited *Delhi: The First City*; *Chennai: A City of Change*; *Hyderabad: A City of Hope*; *Kolkata: A Soul City*; *Lucknow: A City Between Cultures*; *Mumbai: A City of Dreams*; and *Freeing the Spirit: Iconic Women of India*.

Malvika Singh has also worked in theatre and film, and was decorated as a Dame in the civil merit honours list of the King of Spain in 2009.

First published in 2016
by
LIMITED EDITIONS
an imprint of

ACADEMIC FOUNDATION

Delhi Sales Office:
4772-73/23 Bharat Ram Road,
(23 Ansari Road), Darya Ganj,
New Delhi - 110 002 (India).
Tel : +91-11-23245001 / 02.
Fax : +91-11-23245005.

Corporate Office:
No. 35, Sector 7,
IMT Manesar,
Gurgaon - 122050.
Haryana (India).
Tel: +91-124-4215070 / 71.

E-mail : books@academicfoundation.com
www.academicfoundation.org

Ageless India, Book 5
Monumental India
Curated by Abha Narain Lambah

Series Editor: Malvika Singh

ISBN 13: 9789332702059

Designed, printed and bound by
The Book Mint, New Delhi.
www.thebookmint.in